PLANETARY GEAR

TED PEARSON

PLANETARY GEAR

ROOF • NEW YORK

Many of these stanzas were first published in *dark ages clasp the daisy root, furnitures, Hambone, screens and tasted parallels,* and *Temblor.* My thanks to the editors for their support.

ISBN: 0-937804-43-6
Library of Congress Catalog Card No.: 91-67074

Cover design by Deborah Thomas.
Cover art: Still Life, 1928 by A. Rodchenko.

This book was made possible, in part, by grants from the New York State Council on the Arts, The National Endowment for the Arts, and other generous donors.

ROOF BOOKS
are published by
The Segue Foundation
303 East 8th Street
New York, New York 10009

For Larry Price

PLANETARY GEAR

a world lost, a world unsuspected
a song beginning to continue pendent
the whip literally previous the one head
given the many temptations adamant
to stave augment its occasion

of things their confines
and their consorts the ecliptic
debunks grapht echoes to fathom loci
the plectra of annulars
struck from a lune

I began as none other
the figure drawn was this figure
perhaps to recall how it came to be here
by the window in the evening
as the blinds were drawn

who so rutted could fail to explain
the road over and the road back
beyond the poses of delinquent weather
into what pride's remnants reckon

one dimension too many axioms in flux
harmonic meccas harbor tunes
from chords to accord a concordance

gods fettered to gods' eyes
disuse belies their works and wonders
good and twisted the lot of them home
to elsewheres of their own

impenitent of ecstasy the drums of heaven
are companionable makeshift
and older than the wind

bitter cold it was and still
amidst these aspirants that will not surmount
the indefinite no matter
the fact of it

something less than what's more
neither spirit enough nor time
the thing itself a contrivance
sanctuarial ebb of the sea

particular days in a strange land
in winter the form imposed is long
particular words the road another's
and no less particular song

remote devices mano a mano
convened to mediate passion's flower
la lacuna's implacable demon

the inconsequent stare of occasion daunts
inconstant relics of consent
unprepossessing and damned forthwith
the hell of it utterly spent

restless variants otherwise narcotic
inhabit the sentiment of form
blatantly obscene whose life in death
finds shelter from the storm

a child's garden of uncertainty spans
swollen acres of virgin ground
o fractal mood resigned to conclude a goof
or graciousness of love surely

the brickbats of legend unduly mouth
their mothering frags in heat
such duty-free booty to have lived so long
on the sunny side of the street

syntax of place divulges the outward
skin compounded of all that is difficult
lost in coincident waves that break
and rootless make up ground

a rumored anything but random dark
surrounds doucement the world's trial sum
suspended yet animate as if to mark
its fatal medium

a song of the sign but not so simply
to define the anterior edge of time
where none precede the one in tangent
nor otherwise grace its line

equivocal tones in passing though
the eye inclines toward age
uneasy custom my wont or pyre
where found things waken under fire

wired to the was of its slated plot
the guttered pulse of a shuttered other
proposed in song a song to be
reprised in superfluity

a shadow world of hope deferred
or spared the pleasure of living hands
these old walls scoured in retreat

they are stories are they not
these fabled errants of
cloudless night virtual heaven
odds-on paradigms

novae flex for the void they cozen
tempered strange to common ends
crazed sacramentals smoke without fire
true doubles limned portend

each bit prophesies stone proper
to its orbit the world tacitly redounds
to sounds like music makes

triads tithe iconic sections bred
in nascent rifts of sight
sunswept motes of shed effects double down
in earthly delight

escalated music endless steps
tensors sited at the roots of soul
whence these overdriven edges ebb
to constants you condole

the pigment rests on its palette
for want of what's not there
while hand and eye draft substance
from what words were and where

ever another and an other come
to please and to be pleased
detailing thus unwearied lust
a hardness reft of ease

flesh and bone an old saw
left in the traces equally worn
and sung if at all if it cuts

with no thought of the road
save you are on it grammar likewise
devolves on want and wants
what it wants don't ask

under tattooed skulls the color of legend
hips ripple in a royal strut
ten thousand songs and skin's organon
glister and surround me

no good trick derides its mount
in or out of skew
nor reckons echoes of indiscretions of
whole days lost in you

circumstance dances to its own defining
the incised vantage of impatient flesh
on margin each bloom reseeds its hiatus
in a motley of endless arrivals

inscriptions furrowed in fond purlieus
of the foreground's least detent
indite the sun's euphoric bent and shade
each form in kind

under leaden skies the trees grow bare
within a circumference of heavy weather
ever always and already there

thunderation strikes its rites
from the set the vocalic mass uplifted
powers fallen dew

chords prime evil notes airing out the dead
in the sting of morning fingers rate
by rote what's left unsaid

a door barred by sudden others
their sum the measure of a thing like that
and their song a bedlam sans merci
of obligatory weekends in madness

cells in division remainder what
ever else reposes in despair
to bestir a breeze of like unease
within the dissembling air

xenobodacious winds displace us
who with a leg up from eden lope
to the god thang on its reed enwreathed
and dusted slake our gait

parafoibles and bijouteries
adorn the heterologies
of those whose I's historicize
the fabled mind's disease

earth's subaltern charms disdain
the cartographer's passion
for the demi-mondaine he has splayed
for his compass rose

cancelled gravity unearthed remains
a tide starved for mere furtherance
at daybreak on the adamantine natch

random access deplodes the bricoleur
hand-carved shadows knock on wood
indeed we do and you do too
whose hoodoo adoremus

from the chief viscera to the four winds
up late with early bird
later samplings zoned on the daybed
microtonic word

captive mist bridges the moonpath
over ancient scars a tissue of longing
and rivers of unholy commerce

a lame god in glad rags
fashions honey from the bitter grasses
duly anointed my worthy constituents
watch the eagle fly

atomisized flagellants cant ribbed plaints
and ply amidst this widowed thicket
drumabolic ruses

heritable shards shout down accumulation
enough is enough the interminable subject
and the grail of a durable good

sources cited beyond glass panes
on the street the dialects of wind and rain
to redress a moment's heat

snake-hips wail to a planetary jam
in codex the wild rose aspires to its scent
and the updraft takes you higher

the millennium essays its lyric accretions
of angels in equipoise graveyard sex
and changelings thralled to the counterhex
of a moonshine rut in hegira

sweet talk guts the imperial will
whose dap stats rue unsited vitals
the cosine diddles cloven proof
intestate flowers wag

animate edges of the urban oblique
honed on the known if ravaged odds
of logoismo swacked on morphemes
shackled plangent to the regs verdad

vicissitudes galore in drag minor
preclude safe passage over strewn leaves
lost amidst inappreciable mists
and the husks of autumn's interdiction

a simple art in the execution
amps its ardor up to defend
factored seconds against the grain
untended fires portend

mother time in a wilderness voiced
the residuum an earth age
imaged in ash and a ravening
lust for profits

mcjuju crafts its graven drafts
under starry fitments of entropic heat
while day-wage wraiths in aftermath
party hard to a heart's last beat

canny hours becalm the course
the old sod runs to blooded ground
in libidinal troves its limbic source
gets lost before it's found

lexic bytes in idle guises bump
to boot the patrons of hunger
astride an abyss of eventualities
launched by a taunt-laced grind

deadbeats suture a bloodgraft's glyph
to subsistence coded as time's interregnum
awash in eternity's rain

starlight scopes the impolitic venues
kinship staked on the road to hell
the seductive inertia of real numbers
moonglow phased to the tidal swell

seawrack laps the last domain
at issue an epoch of rooms and views
opacities dubbed from their own excess
to a music box of blues

of mechanic hours and a terminal sun
this sedimentary journal logs and flaunts
the griefs and grievances
our habitus haunts

OTHER ROOF BOOKS

Andrews, Bruce. **Getting Ready To Have Been Frightened**. 116p. $7.50.
Andrews, Bruce. **R & B.** 32p. $2.50.
*Andrews, Bruce. **Wobbling.** 96p. $5.
Bee, Susan [Laufer]. **The Occurrence of Tune**, text by Charles Bernstein.
  9 plates, 24p. $6.
Benson, Steve. **Blue Book**. Copub. with The Figures. 250p. $12.50
Bernstein, Charles. **Controlling Interests**. 88p. $6.
Bernstein, Charles (editor). **The Politics of Poetic Form**. 246p. $12.95.
Brossard, Nicole. **Picture Theory**. 188p. $11.95.
Child, Abigail. **From Solids**. 30p. $3.
Davies, Alan. **Active 24 Hours**. 100p. $5.
Davies, Alan. **Signage**. 184p. $11.
Day, Jean. **A Young Recruit**. 58p. $6.
Dickenson, George-Therese. **Transducing**. 175p. $7.50.
Di Palma, Ray. **Raik**. 100p. $9.95.
*Dreyer, Lynne. **The White Museum**. 80p. $6.
Eigner, Larry. **Areas Lights Heights**. 182p. $12, $22 (cloth).
Gizzi, Michael. **Continental Harmonies**. 92p. $8.95.
Gottlieb, Michael. **Ninety-Six Tears**. 88p. $5.
Grenier, Robert. **A Day at the Beach**. 80p. $6.
Hills, Henry. **Making Money**. 72p. $7.50. VHS videotape $24.95.
  Book & tape $29.95.
Inman, P. **Red Shift**. 64p. $6.
Legend. Collaboration by Andrews, Bernstein, DiPalma, McCaffery,
  and Silliman. Copub. with L=A=N=G=U=A=G=E. 250p. $12.
Mac Low, Jackson. **Representative Works: 1938-1985**. 360p. $12.95,
  $18.95 (cloth).
Mac Low, Jackson. **Twenties**. 112p. $8.95.
McCaffery, Steve. **North of Intention**. 240p. $12.95.
Moriarty, Laura. **Rondeaux**. 107p. $8.
Perelman, Bob. **Face Value**. 72p. $6.
*Robinson, Kit. **Ice Cubes**. 96p. $6.
Seaton, Peter. **The Son Master**. 64p. $4.
*Sherry, James. **Part Songs**. 28p. $10.
Sherry, James. **Popular Fiction**. 84p. $6.
Silliman, Ron. **The Age of Huts**. 150p. $10.
Silliman, Ron. **The New Sentence**. 200p. $10.
Templeton, Fiona. **YOU-The City**. 150p. $11.95.
Ward, Diane. Facsimile (Photocopy of **On Duke Ellington's Birthday,
  Trop-I- Dom, The Light American**, and Theory of Emotion). 50p. $5.
*Ward, Diane. **Never Without One**. 72pp. $5.
Ward, Diane. **Relation**. 64p. $7.50.
Watten, Barrett. **Progress**. 122p. $7.50.
Weiner, Hannah. **Little Books/Indians**. 92p. $4.

*Out of Print

For ordering or complete catalog write:
SEGUE DISTRIBUTING, 303 East 8th Street, New York, NY 10009